THE YAHOO! MESSENGER
GUIDE TO ALL THINGS IM

PING!

THE YAHOO! MESSENGER GUIDE TO ALL THINGS IM

A YAHOO! GUIDEBOOK

by Angela Gunn

Sterling Publishing
New York

Published by Sterling Publishing Co., Inc.
387 Park Avenue South, New York, NY 10016

Distributed in Canada by Sterling Publishing
c/o Canadian Manda Group, 165 Dufferin Street
Toronto, Ontario, Canada M6K 3H6

Distributed in Great Britain by Chrysalis Books
64 Brewery Road, London N7 9NT, England

Distributed in Australia by Capricorn Link (Australia) Pty. Ltd.
P.O. Box 704, Windsor, NSW 2756, Australia

ISBN 1-4027-2817-4

Library of Congress Cataloging-in-Publication Data
Gunn, Angela.
Ping! : the Yahoo! : messenger guide to all things instant messaging / by Angela Gunn.— 1st ed.
p. cm.
Includes bibliographical references and index.
ISBN 1-4027-2817-4 (9781402728174)
1. Instant messaging. I. Title. TK5105.73.G86 2005
004.692—dc22 2005009802

1 3 5 7 9 8 6 4 2

Manufactured in China

DEDICATION

To Tara Gelfant for inspiring this book. It's amazing to watch her communicate with fifty of her closest high school friends with just ten fingers.

Big Hug, of course!

Contents

INTRO

U R HERE: WHY INSTANT MESSAGING ROCKS AND HOW TO LOOK LIKE A STAR DOING IT

Instant messaging? As in, not tying up your phone, being able to talk to tons of friends at once, and using the computer for something besides homework? And for free? You mean *that* kind of thing?

We can see you're already convinced. But in case anyone asks—parents, older friends, someone who just crawled out from under a rock—we'd say this: IM is a great way to express yourself and keep in touch with friends near and far. It lets you stay connected without using a lot of time that you don't always have. It's a fun, safe way to communicate with the people who matter to you, and sometimes it helps people express things to each other that are hard to talk about face to face.

Sounds good, right? And it's both easy and fun to use. So why a book? Trust us. We know all the best tips, tricks, shortcuts, and other ways to make your message sessions even better—even more memorable and expressive. (We can also help

you take a break from it all when you absolutely have to—messaging is so smart you don't even have to be sitting by the computer for it to keep you connected.) Besides, there's always more cool stuff to know—can you ever get too much celebrity gossip? Too many photos of you and your friends? Too many great songs? The more you know about what you can do with IM, the better it gets—and the smarter you look when you're showing your friends how to do all the cool stuff.

Now, obviously we're awfully fond of Yahoo! Messenger. Throughout this book, you'll see notes designated **how 2 on Yahoo!**, all about how to use Yahoo! Messenger, which has a lot of nifty things that other types of instant messaging just don't have. That said, we've got plenty to tell you about messaging in general: skills and tips, keeping in touch with friends (and meeting new ones), dos and don'ts for IM happiness, and lots more general messaging wisdom. We want to help you know exactly what to do to make instant messaging all yours—your look, your sound, your ideas, your best tool for keeping in touch and having fun. And we've also included a

handy glossary of terms at the end of the book, where you can find quick definitions for terms in **bold** throughout the book.

It's not just our say-so, either—we asked, oh, a couple million of our closest friends. This book has advice, tips, great

ideas, and memorable moments from Yahoo! Messenger fans who shared their stories with us. Funny convos? Great ideas? Secret emoticons and hidden IM tricks? Stories so embarrassing that you're amazed someone didn't just curl up and die on the spot? Yeah, we've got that.

HOW 2 ON YAHOO!

Looking to liven up your convos? The back cover of this book includes a tear-out "cheat sheet" of hidden emoticons you won't find on Yahoo! Messenger's standard menu. (See chapter 3 to learn more about emoticons and other graphics.)

Little book, lots to talk about—shall we get started? First, we'll need to set you up with IM access on the nearest friendly computer. Right this way…

1

>login: Getting started

There's a lot of stuff you can do with IM once you get rolling. First, though, you've got to put yourself in the game. You'll need three things to get started:

- A way to connect to the Internet—for now, we'll assume you use a computer. (Yes, you *can* do it without. We'll talk about other kinds of messaging gear like cell phones in chapter 5.)
- The right software
- A small but intense burst of creativity

Let's deal with the first two requirements first. The great thing about IM is that you can do it from pretty much any computer that has the right software—and not only is the software free, a lot of computers already have it installed and waiting for you.

If you're on your own computer and don't have the software, it's easy and free to download off the Internet.

how 2 on Yahoo!

Go to http://messenger.yahoo.com and click the Get It Now button.

WHO R U?: YOUR YAHOO! ID

Once you've got the software, you're ready to choose a name for yourself online—your **Yahoo! ID**. If you use Yahoo! for other things—games, e-mail, stuff like that—you have a Yahoo! ID already, and you can also use that for Yahoo! Messenger. (For Yahoo! e-mail users, your Yahoo! ID is the part of your e-mail address before the @ yahoo.com.)

how 2 on Yahoo!

We're going to take you through the ins and outs of getting started on Yahoo! Messenger; however, most IM programs require you to go through the same basic steps. This applies to other IM functions as well, such as finding and contacting buddies. When a feature is unique to Yahoo! Messenger, it's explained in a **how 2 on Yahoo!** box just like this one.

If you don't have a Yahoo! ID yet, this is where that burst of creativity comes in: You're going to make one up. Creativity's important, because as you might imagine, there are a lot of people in the world who share your name, and if one of them has already used the name for *their* ID… well, you're out of luck.

Start by filling out the basic information the system needs to set up your account—name and so on. When you get to the blank that asks for a Yahoo! ID, most people try their name first. If you're interested in using your name, type it in and click the button to make a new account—the system will check if it's available and will report back in a second or two.

If you get lucky, great! If not, this is your chance to create a brand-new you. You'll want to pick a name that says something about you not only now but in the future, because the odds are you're going to stick with this ID for a long, long time. (After all, you saw how hard it was just now to come up with something unique. It'll only get harder in the future, with even more people online.)

If your requested ID is taken, Yahoo! will suggest a few that are available. That ID may have a bunch of random numbers in it, though, and we think you're clever enough to do better.

Plenty of experience (both good and bad) has given us some wisdom on what works and what stinks when you're choosing a Yahoo! ID. See the chart on page 16 for some ideas.

Why do you want to avoid continually changing your ID? Think of your ID like a cell phone number—once you know a friend's number, it's a complete pain when he gets a new one and you have to memorize it and change your speed dial and all. Pick something you can stick with, and then stick with it.

DO	EWW
Use letters, numbers, and underscores 	Don't use your age or your favorite celeb crush. If you're avril_fan_age14 now, what happens next year when you're 15? And what about when Miz Lavigne's over? (Yes, these things happen.)
Try a version of your name with something extra in front—instead of johndoe, you could try mister_johndoe or meet_johndoe. 	Profanity just makes you look stupid—and often as not, the system won't let you use those words in an ID. And why would you want to look sleazy like that anyway?
Include a reference to your favorite hobby or sport (for example, soccer_star_4ever); it'll tell people a little bit about you even before you meet. 	Slang can embarrass you down the road. A friend of ours chose shorty(something) as her name… eight years ago, in junior high. Now it looks really(silly).
Try a second language in which you're fluent (or hope to be!). After all, cute_girl looks plenty stylish as jolie_fille. 	Don't give people too much info—no phone numbers, hometowns, or anything else that's private. Even a last name is probably too much information.

KEEPIN IT ON THE DOWN LOW: YR PASSWORD

You'll need a password, and your password should be something you'll never forget and others will never guess. If anyone figures out your password and knows your ID, they can go online and pretend to be you whenever they like, talking to whomever they please while disguised as you. Nobody will know the difference—and anything they say or do, you could get blamed for. Picture it: your little brother messaging the hottie in your class that you've got a crush on...pretending to be *you*. Could you ever live it down? (And if you think that's bad, wait till you see what has happened to some other Messenger users in chapter 8.)

UH-OH

For Pete's sake, don't use the word password. That's just sad.

The good news is that you're not trying to impress anyone with your password, and that you'll probably change it now and then just to be safe. All you have to do is come up with something you'll remember. Squeeze wordstogether, combine l3tt3rs 4nd numb3r5 or CaPs and lOwErCaSe, and otherwise mix things up.

After that, the registration wants some other details about you. It'll help you choose a "security question" in case you ever forget your password, ask you to read and agree with the basic rules of using the service—no spamming, no messing with people, no hacking—and give you something to type in that'll confirm that you're a real live person looking at the screen.

In a few seconds, the system will send you an e-mail to confirm your info. Be sure to open that e-mail—it's the last step before you get started with this stuff, so best to finish it up right.

And now, you click the sign-in button, the computer checks your ID and password, and…

You're on!

Excellent. You're ready to get in touch with your friends, listen to music, play games, and do all the other great stuff that makes IM so wonderful. But first…

RULES OF THE ROAD

There's no crime in being new at something—everyone's got to start somewhere. But knowing a few basics of Netiquette will help you ease into the scene that much faster. It's kind of like knowing not to wear a tuxedo to a pool party, or whether to call your friend's parents Mr. and Mrs. Whatever or Jeff and Susan. We'll have more pointers for you as we go along, but the two essential rules of Netiquette are:

- Typing in all lowercase letters is fine; TYPING IN ALL-CAPS IS NOT. It's hard to read and *incredibly* annoying—in fact, it's the online equivalent of shouting.
- Try to keep each IM more or less brief. Let your friends get a word in edgewise.

Got that? Good. Let's go find people to hang out with.

2

>sup? Finding yr friends online

Your IM: population 1. Yawn. In this chapter, we'll get your friends into the mix—friends who already do messaging and friends who don't (yet). We'll show you how to set up a list of the folks you most want to keep in touch with, and give you a few tips on how to deal with the rest of the planet.

IT'S WHO U KNOW

You probably already know at least a few people with whom you want to chat on a regular basis: friends, relatives, more friends, cuties you'd like to be friends with, and so on. If you know their Yahoo! IDs, you can put them on your **Messenger List:** a list of Yahoo! IDs that are visible right in the main messaging window. That list gives you not only a handy way of contacting those friends, but lets you see at a glance who's online, who's not, and even what folks are doing while they hang out. (On page 20 you'll find a typical list.)

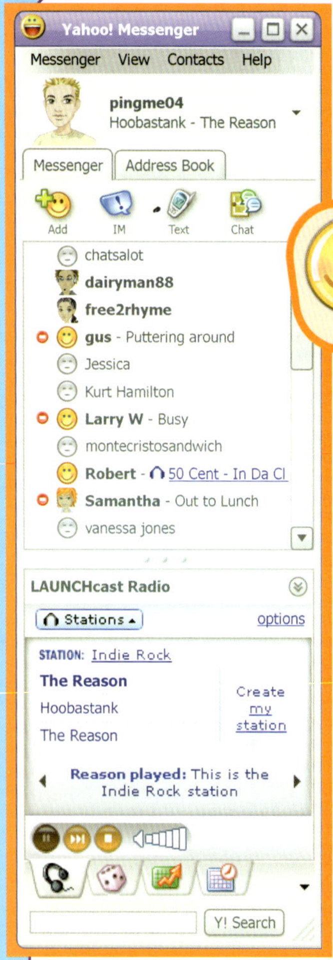

A typical Yahoo! Messenger List

Great, but how do your friends get on your list? You add them. You'll need to know their Yahoo! ID. Click the Add button near the top of the main messaging window and fill in your friend's Yahoo! ID. Messenger will now send your friend a note informing her that you'd like to add her name to your list of messaging friends. If she accepts, her name will appear on your Messenger List.

SORTING IT OUT: GROUPS

A ginormous list of friends is impressive, but grouping your buds in some kind of logical arrangement can help you easily keep track of the people you *really* want to know about at any given time. **Groups** are just a way of keeping a set of names clustered together.

The clusters are up to you—Friends, Family, and

Cuties? School, Soccer Team, and Choir? A, B, C, D, and so on? (Okay, that last one is *really* organized. You scare us.) The groups are visible only to you because they are on *your* Messenger List, so no one needs to know

HOW 2 ON YAHOO!

To add a new Group to your Messenger List, click the Contacts menu in Messenger, select Organize Messenger List and then Create New Group. Enter the name of your new Group and click OK. Drag and drop your current friends' Yahoo! IDs into your new group.

that you've included him or her in a group called Babbling Fools. Groups are strictly a way of keeping your life in order.

HELLO WORLD

The idea of creating customized groups gets us into one of the most incredible things about IM: It's utterly your world, your look, your thing. We're going to show you ways to personalize pretty much every little aspect of messaging, but first let's send and receive a few messages, just to get started.

From your list, pick a friend who's online and available to chat—you can tell because his or her Yahoo! ID appears in **bold**. Double-click on the ID of the person you want to chat with and a window opens. Start typing. Your words will appear in the lower half of the IM window. When you hit the

Send button on the right, the words will shift to the upper window—and appear on your friend's screen. That's it; you have just started a **convo**. Add your friend to a group in your list, if you like, and we'll move on.

STEAL THIS IDEA!

A friend of ours creates a group for every class she has each semester. She gets classmates' IDs and adds them to her list; if she's doing homework and wants to talk it over with someone, all she has to do is see who's online from that class. At the end of the semester, she drags and drops the names back into her main Friends group, then deletes the class-specific group.

GATHER ROUND PPL

Next, it's time to get in touch with people who should be on your list, but whose Yahoo! ID you may not have—yet. The best way to get someone's info is to ask—in person, by e-mail, whatever works for you. IM usernames from other services, like AOL and MSN, will not work with Yahoo! Messenger (although software does exist that links together different services, but that's for more advanced users and outside the scope of this book). If your friend is a Yahoo! Messenger user, great—add them to your list just as you did the others. If they're not, tell them to get with the program!

Messaging is a one-on-one thing—you type, your friend types back, and so on. That said, you can have as many one-on-one conversations at one time as you can handle, making messaging slightly *more* efficient than life offline. Each convo gets its own window. Needless to say, it's crucial to keep track of which one's which—and when we tell you about personalizing your environment in chapter 3, we have a very cool trick to make it at-a-glance simple (see page 37). For now, though, remember that the name of the person you're chatting with appears in the upper-left corner of the window, and their words appear in the top half of the same window.

GeekSpeak

Your Messenger List of friends is server-based—stored with Yahoo! That means that no matter what computer you use to log in, you'll always have your list handy.

The good news: People in different windows can't "hear" each other—you can be talking to Friend A in one window, dishing on him to Friend B in another window, and no one's the wiser. Sometimes, though, you'll want to congregate in one big group. The messaging equivalent of three-way calling is called conferencing, and it can include as many people as you like. You invite each person separately, but when they accept the invite, they all gather to chat in one window, and everyone can see everyone else's messages. This is handy for making plans or working on projects together.

ALL ABOUT U

Now that you've got the basics of messaging down, you'll want to customize IM to behave the way *you* want it to. Let's take a minute to set up your **preferences**. There's lots to do here, and we'll tackle the fancier stuff in the next chapter. For now, you're going to tell Yahoo! Messenger how you want it to act when you walk in the door, so to speak.

HOW 2 ON YAHOO!

You can get to your preferences through the Messenger menu, or via Ctrl-Shift-P.

In Preferences\General, you can set the IM software to automatically start whenever you get on the computer and to automatically sign you in when you fire up your Net connection. This setting is really handy if you have the computer to yourself, and less so if you have to share. Once you've made your choices, click "OK." (You can always change your mind later.)

You're online and messaging now, but there's so much more to do—both to make your messages as individual as you are, and to enjoy all the extras that come with the "basic" messaging gear. In chapter 3 we'll make you both comfortable and gorgeous, and in chapter 4 we'll cover all the stuff you can do with other people online that doesn't necessarily involve typing.

3

represent: Emoticons, IMVironments, Avatars, and more

You've got your basic messaging on, and your friends know how to reach you (and vice versa). Now comes the part where we make you look and sound as amazing online as you are offline. (One more thing to love about messaging: no bad hair days, no spinach in the teeth, no forgot-to-do-laundry-and-wearing-something-that-crawled-out-of-the-bottom-of-the-closet. Online life is good.)

In this chapter, we'll walk through all the ways you can personalize your messages with **skins** that dress up dull windows; **emoticons** that show how you're reacting to a convo; other visuals (Yahoo! calls them **IMVironments**) that express your personal style; and fresh sounds that add fun to the session. In other words, all the stuff that makes your IM perfectly yours.

XPRESS YRSELF: EMOTICONS

When people first started writing to each other online, they complained that even though instant messages and e-mails were like talking to someone face-to-face, you missed a lot when you couldn't see other people's expressions.

Creative types soon started "drawing" little faces with keyboard characters—for instance, using a colon, a hyphen, and a close parenthesis like so :-) to make a face that you could see if you tilted your head to the side. Bizarre creativity followed, until users were doing everything with emoticons from sticking their tongues out at each other to sending roses… *if* the recipient could figure out the codes.

Messaging makes it easier, translating emoticons into the pictures they're meant to represent. (Even better, many of

TO EXPRESS	TYPE IN	AND YOU GET
big grin	:D	
happy	:)	
sad	:(	
don't tell anyone	:-$	
winking	;)	
tongue	:P	
surprise	:-O	

them are animated.) You can add emoticons to your convo by clicking on the smiling face with sunglasses that appears just above your text area during a convo. Or, if you know the keyboard codes, you can type them in and the system will change them into pictures for you. Try a few of the codes on page 26 in any messaging program you like.

But there's more! The back cover of this book (you noticed how it folds out, right?) lists not only the Yahoo! emoticons you can get if you use the set in your convo window (a much, much longer list than on page 26), but a bunch that you get only if you take the time to type them in. Some of our favorite "hidden" emoticons include:

TO EXPRESS	TYPE IN	AND YOU GET
good luck	%%-	
shame on you	[-X	
dancing	\:D/	
coffee	~O)	
peace sign	:)>-	
chatterbox	:-@	
idea	*-:)	
alien	>-)	

sez u

Here are some favorite Yahoo! emoticons, as written in by our users:

Liz Walker, Alabama

My favorite emoticon is the one that yawns. The first time one of my best friends instant messaged it to me, I was really tired so I yawned at the same time...we couldn't stop laughing because I was on webcam when it had happened.

Donna Phipps, Michigan

I like to use the party guy along with the kiss guy. It is like you are blowing a kiss to the person.

Shanice Thomas, New Jersey

When instant messaging my friend who uses the one-finger typing method, I use my favorite emoticons—waiting, yawn, rolling eyes—to tell her to speed it up and stop taking for-ev-er!!! She cannot type to save her life! Thanks guys. I love my Yahoo!

Amanda McCafferty, Pennsylvania

Someone was doing something right when they put a cowboy hat on an emoticon! That one is definitely my favorite.

Sophia T., Minnesota

I like using the hidden emoticons because I can send cool, weird, and funny messages with a personal touch without being too mainstream. Yahoo! Messenger is also cool because you can keep in touch with people from TOSOTW (the other side of the world)!

SHORT & SWEET: ABBREVIATIONS

Messaging fans also use an "**IMspeak**" vocabulary of acronyms and abbreviations, some of which are substitutes

IM SPEAK

2mi (or) tmi	Too much information
btw	By the way
b/w	Between
cya (or) c-ya	See ya
g2g	Got to go *(or, alternately, good to go)*
gv	Go voice *(that is, let's stop doing IM and switch to the phone)*
idk	I don't know
jk	Just kidding
k	OK *(sure it's just one letter shorter, but that's fifty percent less typing!)*
l8r	Later
lol	Laughing out loud
omg	Oh my God!
pls, tnx	Please, thank you
ppl	People
prolly	Probably
sup	What's up?
ttyl	Talk to you later
u, ur, u2	You, you're/your, you too

IM SPEAK

w/e	Whatever
xoxo	Hugs and kisses

for various emoticons and some of which cover other ground. Throwing in IMspeak terms like "btw" (by the way), "rofl" (rolling on the floor laughing, sometimes typed as "rotfl"), and "brb" (be right back) can move the convo along quickly, especially when you're talking to a lot of people at once.

Anything goes as long as you can make yourself understood, but we find ourselves using a lot of the same 'speak over and over—in convos and also throughout this book ("sez u," for instance, is pure IMspeak). We've rounded up the best of the best abbreviations and acronyms, as submitted by Yahoo! users, on page 31.

It's okay, BTW, to type IMspeak in all-caps—the abbreviations are short enough that they don't have that "shouty" feeling to them.

Another way of making IM say what you want it to is to put actions between asterisks (Shift-8 on the keyboard)—instead of saying "I want to give you a big kiss," you'd type *big kiss*. We've also seen folks use an arrow pointing to their name (for example, **angela <— yawning**

HOW 2 ON YAHOO!

To choose or change your image, go to the Messenger menu, then select "Change my display image"—or just type Ctrl-Shift-K.

and stretching to mean "angela is yawning and stretching"). Unlike emoticons, these techniques both appear exactly the same in the messaging window as they do when you type them, but they're useful for getting your point across simply.

sez u

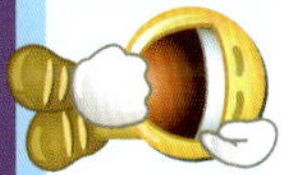

In search of unique IMspeak? Here are fresh abbreviations, courtesy of Yahoo! users:

Gina S., North Carolina
LYLAS=love ya like a sis
BIO=bring it on
BBA8A=be back at 8:00 am

J. Paw, Illinois
LSHIPAL=laughing so hard, I peed a little!

Liz Lefler, Florida
LYMTLI =love you more than life itself

Kristin Ingram, California
IJFOOMCLSIMNAM=I just fell off of my chair laughing so I might need a minute (Yes, sad but true lol)

Larissa B., California
IKURBWAI=I know you are but what am I?

Marlene Caro, New York
SD4YM=save the drama for yo mama

A word of advice: beware of creeping IMspeak. We're hearing a lot lately about people getting in trouble with teachers for using abbreviations in papers and other school assignments. It's funny until you get docked a letter grade. (But then again, what isn't?)

LOOK @ U: DISPLAY IMAGES AND AVATARS

Now that your convos sound like you, let's dress them up. A personalized image or (in Yahoo!) an **Avatar** not only makes the messaging window more fun to look at, it puts your personal style out there for everyone to see.

HOW 2 ON YAHOO!

If you are editing your own images and know how to adjust sizes, they should be 96 pixels square for a large image or 48 pixels square for a small image. If you don't know how to set image sizes, Messenger will set them for you.

DISPLAY IMAGES

Yahoo!'s got a collection of **display images**—little pictures sort of like the icons on your usual computer screen—to start you off, but you'll probably want to branch out. The great news is that the Net is full of creative people who can offer lots of clever examples. Even better, you can turn one of your own images—a photo or something else—into a display image for IM.

You can have as many images as you can fit on your computer's hard drive, and you're not limited to Yahoo!'s picks. The tradeoff is that you can use your display images only on your own computer. If you use Yahoo!, though, there is a way of keeping the same image no matter where you log in to IM: use an Avatar.

AVATARS

Avatars are a special kind of image, and they let you really personalize what other folks see when you're online. You may notice that your friends' Avatars look, well, quite a bit like your actual friends (or at least what your friends like to think they look like, which is cool in its own way—window to the soul and all that). Simply put, Avatars are images created from a virtual wardrobe of body types, skin and hair colors, clothes, accessories, and backdrops.

To personalize your own Avatar (choose its physical appearance, wardrobe, background, and even nifty extras like sports equipment or a pet) right-click and select

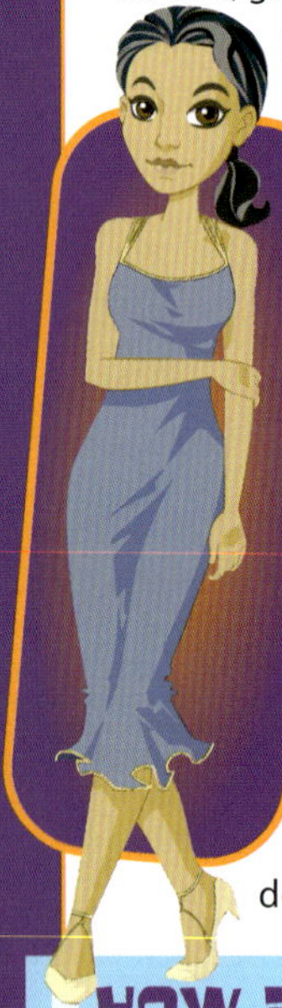

Customize Avatar. (Don't worry; the system will walk you through Avatar creation if you need help.) And because it's all free, getting new clothes and gear for your Avatar can be lots of fun. If you set up an alert (from the main Avatar-creation screen, look near the bottom of the page on the right-hand side), Yahoo! will send you messages when there are new things that'll spiff up your Avatar's closet or surroundings.

Your Avatar, by the way, can do what your emoticons do: express emotion. If you use a 🙂, your Avatar will smile; if you use a ☹, it'll get teary-eyed, and so on. You can also set your Avatar to have a basic general mood—if you don't know which yours ought to have, ask your

HOW 2 ON YAHOO!

If you like, you can switch things up a bit—let some people see your Avatar, some see an image, and others see nothing at all. You can set that for each individual person when you have a convo window open for him or her.

friends. You may learn something interesting about how they see you!

DRESS U UP: SKINS, FONTS, AND IMVIRONMENTS

You now express yourself perfectly, and your Avatar and images are gorgeous—time to do something about that unsightly computer screen.

SKINS

Skins affect how the messenger software looks on your computer (and *only* your computer). To change to a different skin, go into the Preferences window just as we've done before. You can download fresh skins online—though we strongly suggest sticking with the official skins offered by

GEEKSPEAK

Things that exist or change only on your computer are called "local." Skins change the IM interface locally. Images and skins are both stored locally—that is, on your hard drive.

the services themselves, just because they're likely to work better and not have unexpected "extras" such as viruses—and follow the instructions to save them to your hard drive. (Important: Pay attention to where you're downloading those files; if they land in the wrong directory, you'll have to hunt them down.)

If you really want to make an impression on friends,

though, you'll want to spiff up your convo windows—and that means changing your fonts and, in Yahoo!, your IMVironments.

UH-OH

Yellow text on a white background—or any other unreadable format combo—is an invitation for reasonable people to never IM with you again. Because they'll be blind. And it'll be your fault.

FONTS

Let's start with fonts—after all, what do you spend most of your time looking at in a convo? (Hint: If your answer was "emoticons," you're probably overusing them.) You can change the style, size, and color of the words you type in any given convo.

In fact, if you're someone who likes to keep a lot of convos going at once (or if you're one of those super-focused people who can handle a convo and your homework at the same time), sometimes it's useful to keep your convo types looking distinctly different in each case. Bright purple and huge? Why not? You can set it to display that way only to the other person in your convo or conference, and you'll be able to tell at a glance the difference between that and the term-paper window. Or you can make bright-purple-and-huge your signature text format for every convo you have. Your friends certainly won't mistake you for anyone else. Easy to do, too: Look in your convo window between your friend's words up top and your typing area below, and you'll see a T with a painter's palette behind it. You can make a temporary change there, or for something more permanent you can make your choices in Preferences\Appearance\Default Color and Font for Message Windows.

HOW 2 ON YAHOO!

To get to IMVironments from inside a convo window, click the word "IMVironment," which appears just above the space you type in.

IMVIRONMENTS

You can also go one step further in Yahoo!, customizing not just the words but the windows behind them. These are called **IMVironments** and they're sort of like wallpaper (but very animated wallpaper!) for convos. Unlike skins, everyone you IM with can see your IMVironments. All sorts of IMVironments can be checked out in any convo window, and as with fonts you can choose something different for each of your IM friends or you can stick with one signature theme for all your messaging.

And yes, you really can spend as much time coordinating your convo windows as you can choosing your outfit for the day. (But don't you always look fabulous when you put in that kind of effort?)

SOUNDS LIKE FUN: SETTING ALERTS

There's one more extra that can make your convo space all yours: You can tweak the sounds you hear when stuff happens.

All those sounds you hear when things happen in messaging—friends signing on and off, convos beginning and ending, mail arriving, and so on—are controlled in your Preferences window, and you can use either the sound files that come with the program or any sounds you've got stored on the hard drive in a format called WAV. (A lot of computers already use WAV files for their system sounds—the beeps and tunes you hear when you start up, shut down, or get mail.)

If you're craving something unique—from a favorite television show, for instance—you can download more WAV files online and save them to your hard drive to use here (though, again, only when you're at your own computer, since like skins and images, sounds are stored locally). Or you can cut the racket and have no audible alerts whatsoever. As we said before, be careful when downloading from non-official sites; most people are pretty decent, but sometimes someone will try to slip in a virus or other bad-news program with such files.

Adding sound gets us into a whole set of other ways to interact with friends in messaging—ones that let you not only communicate better, but really hang out, listen to music, play games, surf the Net together, and even swap videos. And if you haven't convinced your friends yet to keep up with your rampant online coolness, we can help you meet other folks who share, say, your obsession for pool. Right this way...

4

hey u: Hanging out, hooking up, and cyber

Believe it or not, there's more to messaging than finding people you know and IMing them. (This is convenient, because eventually even *you* might run out of things to talk about.) In this chapter we'll discuss meeting new convo folk and how to hang out online with them—as well as your usual friends—while giving yourselves something to talk about. There are plenty of great ways to hang out and meet folks in IM. You could…

- Listen to music and share your favorite artists and songs
- Challenge someone to a game
- Send cool links to friends for discussion purposes
- Locate chats centered around favorite hobbies or interests
- Barge right up and introduce yourself to a total stranger

HEY DJ

Don't you think knowing what kind of music someone's into tells you a lot about that person? And don't you love getting or giving music recommendations to friends? The major IM services include "radio" stations with tons more to hear than you'll find on an old-fashioned radio. You'll also find more genres, more artists, and (especially on Yahoo! and, to a lesser extent, on other services) more opportunities to hear great new artists based on stuff you already know you like. These stations let you select genres or artists that you like (or that you know nothing about and want to explore). By rating what you hear, the system learns what you like and don't like, and over time adjusts itself to be more you-centric.

HOW 2 ON YAHOO!

You can tell the world what you're singing along to by going to the Preferences tab in the LAUNCHcast Radio section. All you have to do is set up your Preferences to let that song information appear next to your Yahoo! ID in your friends' Messenger Lists. It'll update itself every time the song changes.

But we're talking IM here, not music. One of the great things you can do through Yahoo! Messenger is share your good musical taste with the world—and maybe learn something from someone else's picks as displayed in Messenger.

Letting folks know what you're listening to can be a great conversation starter.

Of course, if you want to show off what you love, you'll have to set up your personal radio station. Yahoo!'s LAUNCHcast Radio is, again, a whole different book, but the basic idea is to go into your personal radio station and start rating songs and artists you love or hate. The more you do, the smarter the system gets about you and the better its music choices. Over time it becomes the kind of radio station you'd program if you, well, owned a radio station.

GAME ON

Music's great, but it's somewhat passive—your friends check out your music or they don't. Adrenaline junkies who think they've got skills are directed to the games area, where they can meet new people to compete with in games ranging from chess to pool. (In Yahoo!, check out the Games logo—the one with the —along the bottom of the main messaging window.)

UH-OH

Careful in the game rooms—the mood varies, and some are so focused on the game itself that chitchat will get you in trouble. Take a minute to scope out the mood of the room before you assume that it's okay to initiate a non-game-related convo. And watch the trash talk until you're sure it's the right atmosphere.

Gaming is one of those things you can do with friends or with people you've never even met—consider it a universal language, if you like. It's a great thing to do if you want to spend time with friends but don't necessarily have a lot to talk about. Pick a game, send a message to your soon-to-be competitor, and get rolling.

This being messaging, talking smack with your friends is not only possible but highly encouraged. One of the best ways to give friends a hard time during a game is to throw an **Audible** at them. Audibles are great little animations with sound, and Yahoo! has all kinds, from sweet to weird.

HOW 2 ON YAHOO!

To check out Audibles: In your convo window, click on the red lips just above your typing space—but pay special attention to the Games section you get if you click the "More Audibles" button. The "Taunts" Audibles are excellent for messing with an opponent's head—after all, if your opponent is laughing, he's just distracted enough to mess with his game. Advantage: You.

SPREAD THE NEWS

Looking for an easy way to share your interests or get your friends involved in a discussion? If you've found a cool link online—gossip about your favorite celeb or something of a more serious nature—put it out there. Consider including a URL in your status message, like so: www.yahoo.com. It'll be clickable, and your friends can follow it to see what you're looking at. (Status messages are discussed more thoroughly in chapter 6.)

HOW 2 ON YAHOO!

Have a cool link you'd like to share with your Messenger List but you don't want a long, messy URL next to your Yahoo! ID? Here's a tip on how to make the link say exactly what you want. Simply type the link, followed by a space, and then the text you'd like to appear next to your name. For example, http://yahoo.com Yahoo! Rocks will look like this:

johnsmith1656 - Yahoo! Rocks

U U U: YR PROFILE

Since this chapter is all about how you're going to dazzle both friends and strangers, you should let the world at large know something about you. Time to set up your profile.

Your profile is a cross between a telephone directory (but for Yahoo! IDs, not phone numbers) and a face book. Use it to tell the world as much or as little about yourself as you like.

Having a Yahoo! ID means automatically having a profile page, but unless you decide to provide some information, all it'll say is that your ID exists. However, you can provide a lot more than that, including favorite quotes, links to sites you like, games you prefer to play, and a note on what's up with you.

You can also indicate whether you want to make this information available to other members.

For now, we suggest not supplying any info that is too personal—last name and location—and loading up on the stuff that'll help interesting people to find you: gender, hobbies, interests, a quote that really sums up who you are (or who you are today at least), and links to sites you care about. You can even upload a photo if you like.

WR THE PPL R: THE DIRECTORY AND CHAT ROOMS

Obviously other people have created profiles before you. If you search the **Member Directory**, you can see what they wrote—and, if you like, introduce yourself.

See someone who sounds like your kind of people? Are they online? Introduce yourself if you like: Send them an IM and ask if they'd like to talk. We recommend that you be specific in your note about why they seem like someone you'd want to get to know.

Where else can you find people? Everywhere. The most obvious choice, of course, is in chat rooms, where others gather for convo purposes—drop in, mix it up, and if you meet someone you like there, invite them to talk some other time. There are those who prefer action to words; shake off the single-player-game habit and many thousands of folk online are just waiting to kick your… um, to get to know you. Show your skills and then strike up a convo.

If you're seriously into your music, it can be fun to look for other Yahoo! Music members who share your music tastes.

LAUNCHcast Radio lets you look for other members who like the things you like and maybe even know about some artists you should know but don't. When the "Fans" selection appears at the bottom of your LAUNCHcast Radio window, click to browse by song, album, or artist. If you find someone whose station consistently blows you away, drop them a friendly note and who knows? Maybe you've got a new IM friend.

A word, though, about your new IM pals. Just because you're having a great convo with someone doesn't mean you know this person. *At all.* Be careful not to give out (or ask for!) personal info—last name, address, phone number, and so forth—and be highly suspicious of anyone who presses you for it. And if anyone wants to meet you in person? The answer is no. That's not what messaging is about.

And if someone asks you to cyber? Well…

2 CYBER OR NO: THOUGHTS

Cybering is something your parents would probably prefer you not know about, let alone do, but we'll speak the truth: Not only is the Net full of opportunities for NC-17-rated convos, odds are you're going to be tempted to cyber at least once or twice. There, we said it.

We're gonna advise you to skip cybering, even though it's just words on a screen. The thing about raunchy convos is that even when you're done having fun, they can linger. With your Yahoo! ID all over them, no less. Maybe you're really close with your honey, maybe you're just pretending, maybe you're just bored and want to shock the convo—but someone who sees it might not understand your motives and start talking about your business where they have no right to.

And how would somebody see a private convo, you ask? In chapter 8 we're going to tell you about a nasty practice called **pickling** and how a perfectly nice person like you could get on the wrong side of something like that. Stay tuned (or see page 83).

UH-OH

Just because your folks don't know the term "cybering" doesn't mean they won't recognize what it is if they find it on your computer, either reading over your shoulder or snooping through a log of your chats.

The other risk of cyber, of course, is ending up in an inappropriate conversation with someone who misled you about his or her age, gender, or appearance. The person on the other side of your chat could be someone you wouldn't want to share so much as a bus ride with!

Now that you know how and what to talk about, isn't your butt getting kind of tired of that desk chair? We thought so. Fortunately, these days you don't have to be plopped down in front of a computer to keep in touch. Instead, there's…

5

yr gear: IM tools that let you always stay in touch

Lots of people own more than one device that can do computer-type tasks, even though you may not think of certain gadgets as computers. In this chapter we'll discuss how to take your habit on the road, using cell phones and other mobile devices. Still stuck behind your computer? Add a little action to the convo with nifty add-ons such as voice chat, which lets you combine IM with actual speaking (but over the Net, not your phone!), and webcams, which add live video to the mix.

GO GO GO

If by now you're seriously addicted to IM—or seriously over dealing with your computer—you may be ready to think about devices that'll let you message without sitting in one place staring at a screen all day. You may even have one: your cell phone, portable game player, or other device could serve this purpose.

Why use something besides a computer to message? Most folks consider the option a convenience—log in, check messages or see who's around, sign off—but we've talked to a number of IMers who rely heavily on non-computer methods of getting and staying online. Their reasons:

- They share a computer with the whole family and using a mobile gadget is cheaper than buying another machine.
- They travel a lot, either each day (long distances to and from school, for instance) or because their relatives are scattered around.
- Activities or jobs keep them out of the house.
- They hate to miss out on a single convo—with a remote hookup they can stay in touch all the time, no matter where they are.

Fair enough, but you still need to make sure you've got gear. If you have a relatively new cell phone—one with Internet capabilities—you're probably set. You also need some fancy typing skills and some adjusting where your cell phone service is concerned.

First, make sure your phone has Net capabilities. (Can you surf the Net on it? There's your answer.) If you're not sure, check the info that came with the phone, or haul it to the store and have them show you the ropes.

Next, make sure you've got the right software in there. Some phones come with the right stuff built in; if not, you can go online and get the stuff you need sent to the phone automatically (see page 49).

TXTING TXTING 123

Basic messaging over a regular phone, which involves hitting the digit buttons to select each letter (hit 2 once for A, twice for B, and so on), is a lot like what's called "**texting**," which is very popular in Europe and Asia. Texting is basically IM through your cell phone, which can get a little complicated—in fact, a lot of the abbreviations and IMspeak we discussed in the last chapter are even more popular over there. Texting has one *huge* advantage over regular messaging in that you can send a message to almost anyone with a cell

HOW 2 ON YAHOO!

To get Yahoo! Messenger for your cell phone, go to mobile.yahoo.com/messenger and choose your carrier and phone from the lists. The system will guide you through the selection process and send the software you need right to your handset.

phone (as opposed to only those with computers). Lots of weird little quirks make it simply a useful backup to the skills you already have.

Teens and young adults in Europe and Japan rely a great deal on texting, in part because they are less likely to have regular computer access and more likely to carry the latest cell phones. In fact, older folk in Japan call texting teens and young adults *oyayubi-zoku*, or "thumb tribes," for the way they're always typing away on the keypads. (For the bonus round, the Japanese word for mobile phone is *keitai*.) Your parents, local geek, or cellular company may call texting "SMS," for Short Messaging Service. Same thing.

Texting and the messaging services that operate as texting have a different rhythm from messaging—you send a message, it leaves your screen, a message comes back, it leaves, and so on—so it can be kind of hard to carry on a normal IM conversation. (In that respect it's a little like e-mail, though with texting you don't usually get to see the earlier parts of the conversation "thread.") Also, phone screens are usually pretty small, so you'll want to keep blather to a minimum. It's no coincidence that a lot of IMspeak got its start in texting, where every character counts.

In fact, not only does every character count, but messages *themselves* count—against your bill. A lot of mobile plans don't include text messaging (or its fancier cousin, multimedia messaging), and a lot more allow only a limited number of messages each month. If you're using your phone to message or IMing someone who does, try to get as much info into one message as you can (keeping in mind that there's usually a limit of 150 or so characters per message). And watch the bill carefully; one chatty session can come back to bite you hard at the end of the month.

ALL ABOUT THE IM

Alternately, if you're in the market for an all-new piece of gear, there are a few on the market that deeply understand your love of messaging—and are designed not to cost you a ton of money. They have names like Sidekick and Ogo, and these IM-centric devices are a lot of fun.

Devices like these, built specifically for surfing the Net, checking e-mail, and instant messaging, often look a lot like phones… but not quite. They use computer-style QWERTY keyboards and have screens that snap or twirl outward.

UH-OH

Do you drive? Don't IM while you're behind the wheel. Don't even check messages when you're rolling. It's even more dangerous than talking on the celly while you drive, not to mention unbelievably pretentious and annoying. If you expect a certain message to be that important, pull the heck over to read it.

Even better, these gadgets come with messaging software (and other goodies like a Web browser and e-mail) already built in. And the carriers that sell them understand that you don't much care about using them as telephones: Most offer either combined phone and data service or a data-only plan that's usually a great bargain compared even with cell service. Is it as good as IMing from a computer? If you tend to have a lot of convos open at once, maybe not (since you can't keep multiple windows visible at the same time), but for speed and mobility, these devices are brilliant.

BTW? Your favorite portable gaming gear may also let you do some basic messaging—sometimes within only a few yards of other users of the same game player, but that's changing and getting better all the time. If you play, keep an eye on the Web site for your favorite gadget (since such improvements are usually announced on those official sites), but don't expect this to sub for a serious IM hookup. Still, it's fun if you've got it handy.

LIGHTS CAMERA ACTION

What about when you're back at your computer? Pimping your machine may be just the thing to kick your messaging up to a different level. We talked in chapter 3 about how to make the on-screen messaging interface gorgeous; now it's time to think about taking the visuals one step further. Enter the webcam.

Got a high-speed (cable or DSL) Net connection? Feel like a star? You might want to hook up an inexpensive webcam to add live video to your convo. It's probably not something you want to do every day (because a world in which you have to look perfect before you so much as sit down in front of a computer is not a world we want to come into being), but if you have far-flung friends or relatives with whom you're keeping in touch primarily through messaging, this could be fun.

A super-cheap webcam can be found at any electronics store, or if you're an eBay enthusiast you should look there for an excellent deal. (The person you're hoping to message with needs a webcam, too, though it doesn't have to be a twin to yours.) Follow the directions to set it up, then fire up Messenger and go into—you guessed it—Preferences to set it up.

We strongly suggest that you restrict access to your 'cam to just people you know, or at the very least to people to

whom you give permission. After all, do you want any random weirdo taking a close-up look at you?

SOUND CHECK

There's one more great option for adding some flair to a messaging session: You can add actual spoken words to your messaging session. (How retro, no?) This is a handy way of saving money on phone calls, particularly if you don't actually carry a phone on a regular basis. It's free and it sounds great!

You'll need speakers and a microphone; if you have them built into your computer already, that'll probably do. Your friend will need similar gear. Your "voice chat" and your IM session can proceed simultaneously, though naturally things will go more smoothly if you've got a high-bandwidth connection.

HOW 2 ON YAHOO!

In a convo, click the large "Call" icon near the top of the window (above where your friend types).

We've taken this messaging thing about as far as we can go for the moment—sometimes, sorry to say, you really do have to unplug entirely. And sometimes you need help getting other people to unplug, or at least to quit trying to IM with you. Let's dig into ways to take a break without causing too much trauma in your IM-happy life.

6

l8r: Taking a break, losing a loser, and signing off with style

You can't live without it, right? Well, sometimes you've got to. In this chapter we'll tell you how to take a break without losing touch (or freaking people out when you, *the ever-present IM deity*, are suddenly nowhere to be found).

We'll give you some tips on how to get a little peace and quiet without shutting messaging down completely, and how to deal with people who stubbornly refuse to disappear at your command. We'll also gaze deeply into one of the universe's great mysteries: the right way to end a convo.

LUV 2 TALK BUT...

There are all kinds of perfectly good reasons you can't chat right this minute. In fact, your messenger program has a few excuses built in for you, though they tend to be of the oh-so-thrilling "I'm away" variety. Choose one of these messages and your friends will be able to tell at a glance that you're not able to talk.

Those built-in messages are handy if you're in a hurry, but don't stop there. You're way more entertaining than that (or else why would all these people want to know what you're doing?). Write your own **status message** and not only will people know why you can't talk right now, they can keep in touch with what you're up to and how you're feeling even without messaging you. (This is much better than coming back to a screen full of "what ru doin" windows.)

HOW 2 ON YAHOO!

Click on the status bar just below the menu bar in Yahoo! Messenger—the one with your name on it—to see a selection of status messages or to compose a new one.

Most stellar status messages fall into one of two categories. The first kind is great not so much because the messages in this category are ultra-clever, but because they're so dang reliable—their humans update them more often than most people draw breath. These messages let you know the user is at breakfast, away at class, around the house, on the celly, at the movies, in homework mode, off to bed—wherever he or she goes, you shall know. If you're the kind of person who is constantly on the move and you can spare a few seconds every so often to keep your status updated, go for it.

On the other hand, maybe you're more creative than constant—or maybe you don't need to have people know where you are every minute of the day. In that case we suggest you make your status as witty and memorable as you are, such as:

kidcyber7 - lost my temper, can't find it anyplace

t–r–e–v–o–r–g - 23 days until my bday!

dinosaurs2find - I'm studying—at least that's what I tell my parents

HOW 2 ON YAHOO!

To write your own status message, click on the button mentioned on page 56 (just below the menu bar), then choose the New Status Message option. Your computer saves your five most recent status messages. Be sure to click the box next to Show Busy Icon.

What to say in your status message? Lots of people put in a short and clever crack about where the day's taking them, but why not use the space to…

•Infect all your friends with a line from that song that's stuck in your head?

•Help the group decision-making process by announcing which movie you'd rather go see tonight before you all get into a long, drawn-out messaging session about it?

•Ask everyone if they have any brainstorms about the calculus homework that's ruining your night?

Sez U

Some of the greatest status messages ever, courtesy of Yahoo! users:

- **Dean Marshall, California** - blowing up the kitchen
- **Sean Squier, Florida** - In witness protection program…back after trial and conviction
- **Josh M., Massachusetts** -the computer is away from me
- **Nick S., California** - riding the ponies outside Wal-Mart, be back when I run out of quarters

•Holler at a friend on her b-day?

•Point folks to a cool Web page you found?

(As discussed on pages 42–43, this is easy to do. In your status, put a space after the previous word, then type the URL. All your friends have to do is click and off they'll go.)

UH-OH

Your status message told us, but we didn't need to know that you're…

- IMing with our archenemy in another window
- Too queasy/gassy/bloated to really share right now
- Busily blogging the blow-by-blow on *Fear Factor*
- At phone number 123-456-7890; best to keep that stuff in actual IMs or e-mail
- 4evah in luv with your snooky-pooky-wookums-hunny-bunny-boo (a simple "hanging out with PersonsName" will do—gack!)

IDLE

If you absolutely forget to set a status message, there's a back-up plan, kind of: **Idle**. Idle lets people know that your computer is on but you haven't done anything there recently. That's great if you just neglected to set your status message, since your friends will see by glancing at your name that you're not active. (You can hide the "how long" you've been idle by changing your settings.) But if you seriously need the time-out, Idle doesn't quite fill the bill. Besides, if you space out and start messing with games or music without adjusting those settings, you're busted—they know you're not really away, just dodging.

WR R U? INVISIBLE AND STEALTH MODES

Of course, there's away and there's "away if person X asks." Messaging can handle those awkward social distinctions by making you **invisible**. Some kinds of messaging software (yes, Yahoo!'s) can also make you invisible to some people but not others, in what's called **stealth** mode.

Huh? Think of it like this. Sometimes you really just want to be somewhere without anyone noticing

HOW 2 ON YAHOO!

Invisibility is another thing you can take care of with that big button under the menu bar. To be stealthy (invisible to a certain person), right-click that person's name in your Messenger List and adjust their Stealth Settings. You can also set up Stealth at the group level if you've been organizing those names as we discussed in chapter 2. (This is a PC-only thing—sorry, Mac lovers.)

you—you're shopping for underwear with your grandmother and would rather be under a rock in a foreign country. That's invisible. Other times, you're fine with some people seeing you but not others—you're having fun acting like a little kid at your baby sister's Chuck E. Cheese birthday party until you see the biggest gossip in your class walk through the door. That's stealth time—you never liked her anyway, but you want to avoid ending up on her list of topics.

Most messaging software will let you choose to start every session in invisible mode until you decide otherwise. That can be handy if a lot of people use your computer—we know some extremely embarrassing stories about people who messaged someone they thought was a friend only to find out that they'd just IMed the details of their scorching-hot date to their friend's mom, who was borrowing the computer and "just happened" to start the messaging software. (Think that's bad? Wait till you get to the horror stories in chapter 8.) Your friends will thank you.

Want to reappear? You can switch invisible or stealth mode off the very same way you switched it on—or, better yet, just update your status message. You're back!

GET LOST: IGNORING PESTS

Every once in a while, someone comes along to whom you want to be invisible until right after the Earth falls into the Sun. Drop that loser with the **Ignore** function, which makes you permanently offline to him or her. Set it once—right-click their name, choose Stealth Settings, and select "Permanently offline"—and that not-so-special person is blocked from ever bothering you with IMs again, leaving you to live your happy messaging life as though they never existed. (Shouldn't life offline be so easy?) For people whose names aren't on your Messenger List, there'll be an "Ignore this contact" button on

STEAL THIS IDEA!

Some people worth ignoring:

- Your ex-sweetie's new sweetie
- Someone you can't stand from your old school
- Strangers who start a convo by asking if you have a webcam
- Someone who's sure you're their long-lost Uncle Ignatz, traveling incognito

the window when they first invite you to IM. Take advantage of the opportunity to forget they ever existed.

There are two kinds of ignoring: You can either list exactly whom you don't want getting in touch with you, and the software can ignore them on your behalf, or you can list exactly whom you do want getting in touch with you (and the computer ignores everyone else).

The person you're ignoring, BTW? Doesn't know any of this is happening. As far as they're concerned, you're just never around. Try to keep a straight face if the subject comes up the next time that person runs into you.

DEALIN WITH IM HURTS

Some people we've talked to say that ignoring someone and blocking their messages seem pretty extreme to them; one Web site we visited even claimed it was "worse than murder." Oh please. Ignore can be your friend, especially if you're getting really weird stuff from people you don't know. In fact, strangers who make you truly uncomfortable or try to pry into your offline life should be blocked—and if the harassment (because that's what it is) keeps up, tell a parent or trusted adult. It's totally unacceptable behavior and they don't deserve one bit of your attention.

And if the shoe is on the other foot if you're trying to reach someone who's away or perhaps invisible remain calm, leave a message or two, and get on with your life. Popping out a whole string of queries because you think someone's just lurking or otherwise blowing you off looks incredibly pathetic. Some folks call that a **sendstorm**. Most would call it a way to get yourself ignored, at least temporarily.

Besides, what if you accidentally said something really profound and they're just sitting there thinking about it? Don't you want to give them some room to appreciate the incredible wit and wisdom of You? Of course, what probably happened is that they've stepped out of the room and forgot to mention it, which brings us to…

BYE! BYE! BYE! BYE! BYE! BYE!

Like all good things, every messaging session must end eventually. Problem is, it's not always easy to tell when a conversation's over or just on pause. And let's be honest—some people say goodbye and just keeeeeep talking.

The simplest way to end a convo is to say bye or c-ya or l8r—once. And then quit typing. If you're planning to shut down your messaging program entirely, give the other party thirty seconds or so to say his or her own goodbye, then close up shop.

What if someone just stops talking? Check the window to see if they're still typing or have entered any text. If not, it's possible they've been called away from their computer and didn't have time to let you know. Leave the window open or minimized if you like—if they eventually answer, you'll hear or see the alert—but there's no need to say anything if you want to go away or shut down. Some people just don't say goodbye in IM, just like some people don't say goodbye at the end of a phone call.

STEAL THIS IDEA!

One of the people who worked on this book has a secret code that she and her mom use when they have to quit IMing immediately. If one or the other of them types 123, that's it—no need to explain, just gotta go.

Still, try not to be that person. At least with the phone, you can tell that the call has been disconnected. With messaging, there you sit. And yes, your friends will think you're kind of a jerk if you make a habit of doing it.

IM CONVO - 1

mra_k_l_fullmar: ok, back to homework. c-ya!
chatsalot77: me too – bye!

What's the worst thing you can do? Not stop. A never-ending series of goodbyes is kind of cute when you're on the phone with your sweetie (though not so much for anyone who hears you going on like that). When you're messaging, though, it's a huge waste of time. How can someone miss you if you won't go away?

Interestingly, some of the people who find it hardest to politely conclude a convo online are the same people who expect you to have good manners offline—your parents, older friends, and so on. Which leads us to…

7

Hi Mom!: Dealing with parents, teachers, and other IM aliens

They're out there, you know—wandering around in cyberspace, just waiting to pounce and embarrass you in front of the entire Internet. And they have no idea how ridiculous they look. And they invade your personal privacy. Is life with grownups ever fair?

Oh, *stop* that. Dealing with adults online can be a little weird, but it can also help you to relate to them on a completely different level—one where teens are treated less like immature kids and more like the reasonable, regular human beings they are. And you may find that some of the adults in your life are a lot easier to talk with when the heart-to-heart happens keyboard-to-keyboard.

Of course, you probably don't want your adults prying into every aspect of your online life, and we can help you figure out when to keep them in the loop—and how to get them to step off when you need air. The first half of this chapter describes how to talk with adults using IM, and the second covers how to talk with adults about IM.

ADULT EDUCATION

By now, we bet you use messaging a lot—maybe even more than the phone—and that most of your friends do, too. Odds are that's not true for the grownups in your life, so you may find that you're a lot more knowledgeable about this thing than they are. Be gracious about that, and keep a few tips in mind to help things go smoothly when you find yourself talking to a parent, teacher, or coach online.

First, you're used to juggling a dozen IM windows at once. They're not. If you're distracted and don't keep up your end of the convo somewhat promptly, they're going to ask what you're up to over there and if you're "paying attention." (As you know, many parents don't understand how their kids can manage to do a dozen things at once.) Conversely, if you're a speed typist and they're super-slow, have mercy—write shorter messages, and let them answer one before firing off ten more. They're not used to the rhythm of IM life, and what seems normal to you may strike them as rude or stressful or just too much to handle.

Second, u may think typoes & abbvs r np, but adults tend to care *a lot*. Sticking with your usual all-lowercase style is fine, but dial down the grammar and spelling shortcuts, especially if it's someone from school or a job on the other end of the convo. Adults tend to judge written conversation—letters, e-mail, and now IMs—in part by how "correct" it is, meaning how well it conforms to the structures of formal written

English. It doesn't have to be term-paper-perfect, but you should definitely lean that way. (You should, in turn, politely encourage adults not to type in all caps if they're doing so; they may not realize they're shouting.)

sez u

According to Janna Humphreys, a parent in California:

While I am at work and my son is at school we stay connected via IM. His teacher has Yahoo! Messenger loaded onto the computer in the classroom, so whenever my son needs to contact me he is able to send me an instant message and we chat if time allows. When the teacher needs to tell me how my son is behaving or if he needs to have a parent conference, he can do so with Yahoo! Messenger. This close connection has helped my son to stay in school, stay out of trouble, and we have a great trust with each other.

Third, just as you cringe when you hear your mom or dad try to use the same slang you and your friends do, avoid using too much IMspeak in your exchanges lest they start picking up the habit. It's a little annoying, sure, but if you type out "to" instead of "2," "are you" instead of "ru," and so on, you'll be spared having to explain what each one means—or, worse,

Steal This Idea!

Our friend's brother lives in another town, and a misunderstanding between the two left everyone a little frosty. One night when they were both online, our friend's mom happened to sign on—and, wanting to mend the trouble, invited them both into a conference. They got it all talked out and peace was restored to the family.

having them figure it out and start using IMspeak too often and incorrectly.

Finally, encourage adults to use emoticons and IM's other "extras" to communicate what they may have trouble putting into words. Someone who doesn't know about emoticons might sit there for forty-five seconds looking for a way to explain that something she said is just a joke, where an experienced IM user like you would just throw in a  and keep going. Precision in speech is important in life, sure—but this is off-the-cuff stuff, not an Academy Award–winning screenplay you're crafting. If you can help them express themselves, they're more likely to treat IM as a useful way to communicate, and to respect your use of it as well.

DIPLOMATIC RELATIONS

Introducing your grownups to the fun parts of messaging—emoticons and whatnot—can also assist you in communicating in other ways. The great thing about emoticons and other add-ons is that they both help people express themselves and keep things light, which can in turn encourage you to have the kinds of conversations that are sometimes easier when you're not in the same room. (There are laughing and weeping emoticons, but to date there is no scream-insults-and-run-to-your-room-and-slam-the-door emoticon. This is probably for the best.)

We're not saying you should retreat to IM and avoid dealing with your parents or other adults in person. You shouldn't and you can't. But all the things that make IM different from other kinds of communication—the necessity to explain your thoughts clearly with words, the ability to pause and think before you respond, the chance to snarl under your breath a

sez u

Yahoo! user Tabatha Cruz in Texas writes in:

"I have a friend who hates confronting me when there is a problem between us. He can't seem to talk to me face to face. Instant messaging has provided him with a way of saying what he has to say when he can't express it. We have yelled at each other, made up, expressed our innermost thoughts, and enforced our friendship through instant messaging. Thanks, Yahoo! Messenger, for letting us PING ourselves out of uncomfortable situations when words said are not as effective as words typed."

little bit without being heard—can all work in your favor. You may be a lot more comfortable in IM than the adults in your life, but it's still relatively neutral ground for both of you. If you're having a tough time communicating with a teacher or parent and would like to try a different approach to conversation, suggest taking the convo to IM—set a time, offer to help them get connected, and make it happen.

RESPONDING TO PARENTAL FEARS

Odds are good that you're much more experienced with messaging and the Net than most of the adults in your life. The Internet became popular only about ten years ago, and messaging got big even later, so the stuff that's just part of normal life to you is still a little "out there" to most of them. Worse, they may have heard a lot of horror stories about teens (and younger kids) getting into big trouble by exchanging messages with the Wrong Kind of People.

All this can make your parents a little too interested in your messaging habits, at least as far as you're concerned. They may not understand that messaging is an important part of ordinary teen social life—and something you can do without borrowing the car, hanging out at the mall, going to parties, or making them chauffeur you around. They may be worried about the people you message with, and they may be worried that they don't understand what you're doing or saying up there. (Yes, keeping them out of IMspeak has its disadvantages.) Your job is to get yourself a little privacy while keeping the 'rents calm about what it is you're doing.

Believe it or not, what looks like general parental meddling is usually targeting pretty specific things—they just may not be comfortable expressing those issues to you. Submitted for your consideration, a list of their (probable) worries and what you need to do to let the air out of 'em:

They worry that: You're meeting weirdos online, particularly adults with bad intentions.

You respond by:
•Explaining that you never give out personal information (full name, address, phone number) to anyone you don't already know in person from some non-IM context
•Promising never to arrange to meet anyone you know only from IM
•Showing them your groups and pointing out the Yahoo! IDs of people they know
•Showing them how the Ignore function can get unknown message senders out of your life with just one click

They worry that: IM is a waste of time.

You respond by:
•Reading them the intro to this book, which lays out the advantages
•Having them talk with a teacher, a friend's parent, or other IM-savvy adult
•Discussing how IM fits in with other chillout activities like hanging with friends or watching TV

They worry that: You're spending too much time on the computer.

You respond by:

•Working out a schedule (but reminding them that you use IM to talk with other people in your class about homework; if your teachers make themselves available to talk on IM, tell them about that, too)

•Asking for a message-savvy cell phone or other device like those we talked about in chapter 5

Needless to say, be honest. If you think that what your folks don't know won't hurt them, remember that a lot of parents are getting pretty savvy about monitoring their kids' computer use. If they catch you in a lie, you're liable to lose your Net access, along with whatever trust they did have in you.

U NEED YR SPACE

You're happy to clue in your parents as to what IM's all about, but you—and the friends with whom you chat—need and deserve some privacy, too. Remembering that IM has about as much intrinsic privacy as a postcard sent through the mail, consider working out a system with your friends, either in person or via e-mail, that'll let you talk about sensitive topics without being quite so obvious.

Code names for hotties? Those shouldn't be too tough to figure out—teachers, too. We suggest that while you're working

Sez U

Tony Gaeta, Missouri

I was chatting with my friends via Yahoo! Messenger; and we were using the talk feature with our microphones. I had a movie on in the background. I asked them to hang on for a couple of minutes while I ran down the street. It turns out that I left my microphone on in the chat room. There was a scene in the movie I was watching where a person broke into a house by breaking a window. My friends heard the shattering glass through Yahoo's talk feature and were kinda frazzled. Then the scene proceeded with two men trashing up the room and of course my friends were thinking that my house was being broken into. So one of them actually called the police after getting no response to the several instant messages they sent. When I got back, two cop cars pulled in behind me and thought that I was trying to break into my own house. It took me 45 minutes to clear everything up. We all had a good laugh after that and we still bring up that moment to this day.

SEZ U

Meghan M., Kansas

I love to spend a lot of time in chat rooms. One day I had my hands-free microphone on, and I had been drinking a pop. I totally forgot I had voice chat on and I started a belching contest with my brother in the other room. Needless to say, I beat him, not to mention grossed out a few people.

those out in loving or loathsome detail, you should also think up a few basic, quick-to-type signals for the following:

- Parent nearby (trust us, most of them have figured out *pos* as "parent over shoulder"—and some adults might mistake it for that other phrase that begins "piece of…")
- Gotta go, no time for goodbyes (remember our friend's *123* trick from chapter 6? We've also seen people use "O," for "over.")
- Let's clear this up on the phone/offline
- Change the subject and make it look like we're discussing something else, fast! (This is less suspicious, by the way, than shutting down the chat window when someone walks in.)
- Can't talk now

Having some basic "private language"—the equivalent of being able to make eye contact with a friend at a party and signaling it's time for both of you to make a quick getaway—

will smooth things out if you suddenly haven't got as much peace and quiet as you'd like.

Privacy is great during convos, but occasionally you want privacy after a convo—the kind of privacy you get when you crawl under a rock at the bottom of the ocean. Sometimes a messaging session goes off the rails and crashes into your personal Hall of Shame. And guess what? We asked around, and if you thought you had a prize-winning recipe for making a fool of yourself, wait till you hear about…

8

o no u didnt: When convos go bad… or worse

Everyone's made a fool of themselves in public at least once in his or her life. When you do it online, the good news is that no one can see you turn red and hide under the carpet. The bad news is that the whole incident may have a much longer lifespan than it would if you'd simply fallen on your face in the school cafeteria.

Fortunately, the rest of the Internet is way ahead of you in the stupid-human-tricks department. We've included tales of woe from fellow IMers: Read their sad stories and learn from their humiliation.

And to get you out of those really tough jams, we've included some useful tips for exercising the necessary damage control. Hopefully none of these sad scenarios will happen to you, but if they do, you'll be ready.

PUBLIC EMBARRASSMENT: HUMILIATING YTPO... TYPP... TYPOS

UH-OH RATING: 😮

So you're rolling along, typing at your usual four thousand words per minute, when suddenly your friend's filling the screen with ROTFLs. You didn't say anything funny…or did you? Scroll back…OMG. Stupid typing fingers! That's gotta hurt.

What to do: Laugh it off. Acknowledge your typo, retype, and move on. That even goes for mistyping a Yahoo! ID and sending a message to some stranger—beg pardon for the interruption and roll on. If they get weird about it you can always hit Ignore.

I WAS AN ONLINE GROUPIE: STUPID STALKER TRICKS

UH-OH RATING: 😮 😮

We don't mean real live threat-from-the-Net stalkers. Those qualify as a genuine emergency far beyond the scope of small, brightly colored books. As we've said a few times before, anytime someone you've been dealing with online—particularly someone you've interacted with *only* online—starts acting weird and trying to get into your offline life, it's time to take matters to your parents or another trustworthy adult.

However, there's still room in the world for lovesick fools—specifically, you—to make themselves look like groupies without actually being dangerous to anything besides their own pride. For example, you and your ex-sweetie are still on each other's Messenger Lists. One day you're sitting around, feeling kind of lonely, and before you know what you're doing, you send a semi-mushy message about the good times. And get no response. So you send another, joking about the first message. And get no response. But you can see the name right there on your list of who's online, so you send over an IM asking if you've offended. And get no response. Which upsets you, so you send another IM...

What to do: Back up. We mean that literally—*back away from the keyboard*. You are in the process of thoroughly embarrassing yourself. Barraging someone with messages looks beyond pathetic. Don't even bother sending one more message of apology—not now, anyway. First, switch yourself to "Away" (perhaps with a message that says "Off getting a grip") and do something that takes you away from the computer.

If you've got all this unvented emotion, we suggest you write it down in a journal or something, but not on the computer. You want to prevent yourself from any possible way of making a greater fool of yourself—and a sendstorm like this on your part could lead to your getting pickled by your former sweetie. (And what's **pickling**, and how bad could that be? Keep reading. If you think you've got it bad now...)

Once you're regained control of your senses, return to the computer. If your recipient hasn't yet set her or his system to ignore you, count your blessings and compose an e-mail—a brief, calm e-mail apologizing for the outburst and saying that you'll wait to hear from them before getting in touch again. And keep that promise. If you have reason to think you've been put on his or her Ignore list, skip the e-mail. Ask a mutual friend to deliver an apology on your behalf, again stating that you're truly sorry and won't attempt to make contact again till you hear from them. And keep that promise.

UH-OH

According to Yahoo! user Jessica C. in Texas:

I pinged one boyfriend with a message for the other boyfriend! Needless to say I was minus one boyfriend when that conversation was over.

SORRY, WRONG WINDOW: MIXING UP CHATS

UH-OH RATING:

Usually when you're talking to friends in person, you can tell one from the other without ever having to double-check. However, if you're juggling quite a few convos at once, you may forget exactly where you were typing—that is, until you hit Send on that message moaning about your biology grades to your best friend…which you just typed in the window where you've been chatting with your grandmother about how perfectly school's going. Oops.

What to do: If it's a fairly simple error—just one random message dropped into another convo—apologize and explain what happened; it's really not much more significant than calling someone by the wrong name during a face-to-face conversation. (If you managed to drop an insult onto the wrong window, apologize profusely and tell the recipient what happened. Perhaps you shouldn't be doing multiple convos when you're that upset.)

If, however, you've just said something that never should have been "overheard" by the person in question (a secret or something that exposes a prior lie you told that person), you can try to talk your way out of it or you can apologize.

The truth is a good choice. If you were just blowing off steam about that bio class, tell your grandmother that and reassure her, truthfully and in detail, that your grades are just fine. (If you were just trying to help your friend feel better, she's apt to understand your logic.)

If you were lying, remember that confession is good for the soul. However, this would be a smart time to put all your effort into the conversation into which you dropped that bomb. Tell your other convo friend or friends that you have to do some damage control and that you'll catch up with them later.

PICKLED!

UH-OH RATING:

So you said some pretty shocking/juicy/mean/raunchy things in that convo one night—and now the whole thing's reposted ("pickled") online, complete with your Yahoo! ID.

What to do when your should-have-stayed-private convo goes Web-wide?

What to do: Unfortunately, you may have a tough time living this one down. Once something's on the Net, it can live more or less forever (even if you can convince the so-called friend who posted the convo to take it offline). And it's usually the stuff that started when you were up to no good yourself; maybe you were sendstorming someone you were desperate to talk to, or you were taking a little too much joy in trashing somebody you were upset with that day.

The good news is that most convos are really juicy or scandalous only to the people directly involved with them. If you said something nasty about someone who has a good chance of seeing it, consider a preliminary apology, but otherwise it may be better to chalk it up to a lesson learned the hard way. Drop the so-called friend who pickled you and be more careful in the future.

By the way, you should be careful about saving archives of your convos even on your own computer. Sure they're fun

HOW 2 ON YAHOO!

If you're a Windows user and have chosen to enable convo-logging in Preferences\Archive, you'll find your messages in C:\Program Files\Yahoo!\Messenger\Profiles\yourscreenname\Archive. You can also see them in the software itself by checking under Contacts\Message Archive.

to read later on, but anyone rummaging around in there—whether by hacking or just by sitting at your keyboard when you're not around—can open the file and see heaven knows what. At the very least, store that stale thing somewhere a little less obvious.

HOW TO LOSE A FRIEND IN JUST ONE CONVO

UH-OH RATING:

The great thing about instant messaging is that you have a second to think before you type, but that sure doesn't stop some people from saying the first thing that comes to mind. Sometimes that's fine—doesn't everyone have one friend that blurts out more or less everything that crosses his or her tiny mind? But sometimes a remark that would be simply harsh in person can turn into a friendship-killer on IM.

What to do: If the person you've just offended is actually in a convo with you, stop everything and apologize. Immediately. There'll be time to explain what you meant later, but the first order of business is to apologize for saying something insensitive or offensive. That's not a form of cowardice or denial; it's simply an acknowledgment that something has happened that has upset the dynamic, however unintentionally.

Next, ask if you can stop messaging for a few minutes and talk things out over the phone or in person. Either one will give you more opportunities (tone of voice, body language, bouquet of flowers) to convey nonverbally how seriously you're taking this and how sincere your attempts to mend fences are. If that's a possibility, sign off, take a few deep breaths to compose yourself, and get on with the friendship-mending process.

If your friend has signed off (or put you on Ignore already), make a phone call or send an e-mail with, again, a sincere apology for causing mayhem and an invitation to sit down offline and hash things out. If you feel the need to clarify what you were saying, proceed carefully so as not to dig yourself a deeper hole. Ask questions such as, "How could I have been more tactful or handled that convo better?"

WHO ARE YOU? WHO AM I?: RIGHT CONVO, WRONG PERSON

UH-OH RATING: 😮 😮 😮

You thought your password was safe, but what's this? Your little brother? At your computer? In a convo with your best friend's sweetie? Pretending to be you? *Declaring "your" undying love?!*

What to do: Your parents are going to notice sooner or later if you kill the brat, so forget it—just get him away from the computer as quickly as possible. Do not close the convo. You're going to type exactly one more line, and that line will be something along the lines of *"dude ha u got punkd bobby OUT"* (substituting the name of your wretched brother or sister for Bobby's, of course). After that, hit the phones—you need to place a damage-control call to your best friend. Ask her to get onto Messenger. You're going to explain before she hears about the convo from someone else, and you're going to offer to send your friend the log of the convo if she wants to see what was said. Transparency is smart—if you offer all the details on what happened, your friend's got to be a loser not to give you the benefit of trusting your honesty. However, offering to have your brother shipped to the nearest sewage-treatment plant may be overkill. (Not that

UH-OH

According to Yahoo! user, Lauren H. in Texas:

Once I was talking to one of my friends on Yahoo! and a guy that I knew from school entered the conversation. All three of us started to talk until my friend left. When it was just the two of us, we started to talk about some of the kids at school. He asked me if I had any crushes. I told him about a crush I had and out of nowhere he said "Busted! I'm telling Mom." It was actually my brother filling in for the guy that I knew (he was at his house). The next day everybody knew about the conversation. Oops!

we blame you.) If your friend's comfortable with the idea, you can send a note to The Sweetie apologizing for your idiot sibling, but don't make it look like you're trying to get in touch on the sly. Let things cool down, and when you are calmer you should mention to your parents that Junior has some shaky ethics about impersonating other people online.

Do we even have to tell you after this to change your password, and to avoid using the automatic-login feature if the brat's going to have access to the computer you use for messaging? (See page 89 to learn how to change your password. And make sure to keep your password to yourself!)

HACK ATTACK

UH-OH RATING:

So you were sitting there, minding your own business, and in comes a message from someone you don't know inviting you to click on a cool link. Unfortunately, you did, and suddenly your computer's doing weird stuff and all kinds of ads are popping up without your doing anything. Or maybe you got an e-mail that said your password was about to expire, and to follow a link to renew it. When you got there, the page asked for your current ID and password, and you typed it in…

Bad news: You've probably just been **hacked** or **phished**. The scary thing about hackers, phishers (people who trick others into giving out personal information), and their disgusting ilk is that all you have to do to get hurt by them is to be a friendly or trusting person. It's true and it's rotten, but it's also relatively easy to prevent if you take basic precautions.

What to do: Never, ever click on a link in a message sent to you by someone you don't know. (In fact, some folks recommend not clicking on any link you weren't specifically expecting to get.) In the case of virus infection, which is mainly a problem for users of machines that run Windows, you should make a point of downloading a good antivirus program and keeping it up to date—in fact, that's good policy for anyone who uses the Internet. (If you have high-speed Net access, you should also look into getting a good firewall program, or using the one built into certain systems such as Windows XP.)

HOW 2 ON YAHOO!

To change your password, click on the Yahoo! Account Info option in the Messenger menu or got to http://messenger.yahoo.com and click on "My Account." For more information on lots of ways to protect your personal information and account, check out http://security.yahoo.com—it's always as up to date as possible.

On the whole, this is a conversation you'll want to have with your parents or whomever owns the computer you use. They may be upset that the situation has arisen, but remind them how much better it is that you spoke up right away instead of letting something fester in the machine.

As for phishing: If you think someone's just stolen your password, *change it right away*. And remember, no one with good intentions will ever ask you for your password or security question.

Needless to say, we hope that, like most folks, none of this stuff ever happens to you—that you're just a curious reader who's chosen to hang out with us for the entire length of the book.

Because guess what? We're there! If this were an actual offline class in messaging, you'd be walking out the door of the classroom laughing about how well you did on the final…and figuring out how soon you could compare notes about the experience with your friends on IM.

c-ya!

GLOSSARY

ALERTS: Sounds that get your attention when a certain event occurs. You can set up alerts to tell you when you receive mail, when a friend comes online or goes offline, when you get an IM, and so on.

AVATARS: An Avatar is a full-body representation of you. Dress yourself up and accessorize yourself to express who you are and what you look like. Yahoo! Avatars express emotions by making the face of the emoticons you use in your IM conversation. Compare *images* and *icons*.

CONVO: Short for conversation, particularly an instant messaging conversation

DISPLAY IMAGES: See *images*.

EMOTICONS: When you're IMing with a friend, you can send them a graphic to show them how you're feeling. These graphics are called "emoticons," because they enhance your words with emotions.

GROUPS: In your Yahoo! Messenger List, a group of your friends' IDs under a heading such as *Friends and Family*, *Classmates*, *Soccer Team*, or anything else that helps you keep your list organized. You choose your group names, and only you can see them.

HACKING: Formerly, exploring how a computer or computer system works. These days, however, the word is also used to describe people who try to invade others' computers or systems for bad purposes. Compare *phishing*.

ICONS: Generally, icons are the small pictures on your computer screen that you click to start programs or open files (that is, they're part of the computer or a program you use), but some people refer to the IM images you choose for yourself as icons too. Compare *avatars* and *images*.

IDLE: When you're logged into instant messaging but haven't typed anything in for a while, the system can automatically display an *Idle* message to let your friends know you may have stepped away.

IGNORE: The ability to tell the IM service that you don't want to receive messages from a screen name you're avoiding. It's helpful for blowing off people you don't want to deal with, for now or for keeps.

IMAGES: A picture your friends can see that you choose to appear next to your typing area in an IM convo. Yahoo! images come in two sizes, 48x48 pixels or 96x96 pixels. Compare *avatars* and *icons*.

IMSPEAK: Emoticons ([insert a smiling emoticon]) , abbreviations ("OMG!") and slang ("convo") that give instant messaging its own flavor.

IMVIRONMENTS: A themed environment that accompanies your instant messages. It can be used to convey a feeling or emotion; play interactive games; or share exclusive photos, music, and other forms of media.

INVISIBLE: When you're online, but no one knows it. If you choose to appear invisible in IM, people who have your

name on their Messenger List will think you're offline. You can receive messages even when you are invisible.

MEMBER DIRECTORY: On Yahoo! Messenger, a huge list of peoples' Yahoo! IDs along with personal information they wish to reveal to the world at large. A Directory listing might include info about your hobbies or your favorite classes in school, but avoid giving out really personal stuff like your age, location, or last name.

MESSENGER LIST: Your personal list of friends who also use the IM service. It appears in your Messenger window, and from it you can see who's online and (sometimes) what they're doing.

MOBILE: On the hoof! Mobile access to instant messaging lets you use IM to keep in touch even when you're not on the computer, thanks to cell phones or through IM-centric gadgets such as the Ogo.

PHISHING: Trying to convince someone to reveal passwords, bank info, credit-card numbers, or other info that is secret or personal, usually in hopes of stealing from the victim. Many people consider this a form of hacking called "social engineering."

PREFERENCES: All the options you can set that make Yahoo! Messenger behave exactly the way you want it to—everything from who can holler at you to what sound the computer makes when stuff happens.

PROFILE: A page of information you choose to give out about yourself; may include photos, quotes, biographical info, and more

SENDSTORM: A messaging blitz; sending someone so many IMs they can't keep up

SKINS: Downloadable add-ons that change the look of software so you can coordinate it with other stuff on your screen. (Skins don't change how the program works, though.)

SPIM, SPIMMER: Spam (the equivalent of "junk mail") over instant messaging

STATUS MESSAGE: A message that appears next to your name on others' Messenger Lists. Status messages can tell others you are busy, show what song you're listening to, or share a favorite URL.

STEALTH: A way of logging into instant messaging without letting the people on your list know that you're online. A stealth setting of online or offline can be activated for an entire group or individual contacts. Compare *invisible*.

TEXTING: Specifically, sending instant messages via telephone over a service called "SMS" (short messaging service). Texting can send messages between any two text-ready phones, but it often costs a few cents for each message sent.

YAHOO! ID: Sometimes called a username, account name, or screen name, this is the unique set of letters and numbers that identifies you on Yahoo! In an e-mail address, it's the part before the @ sign—for example, *free2rhyme@yahoo.com* has the Yahoo! ID *free2rhyme*.

ACKNOWLEDGMENTS

Permanent Messenger List status to: The genius Yahoo! team (Jason Anello, Linda Jane Bennett, Britton Glasser, Patrick Crane, Michael Landau, and most especially the mighty Laura Campbell). Special thanks as well to Meredith Peters, Michael Fragnito, Jeffrey Batzli, Kevin Baier, John Leonhardt, Dan Lish, Larry Smith, Arminda Thomas, Tony Fascé, Rob Stumpf—and Grandma, Darrin, Angel, and Mom.

ABOUT THE AUTHOR

An instant messaging addict for over a decade, Angela Gunn co-hosts *PC World's Digital Duo* on PBS and is a columnist for USAToday.com. She co-founded *Yahoo! Internet Life* magazine and writes regularly about technology, culture, ethics, and whatever else amuses her. She lives in New York and Seattle.